Office of the Comptroller of the Currency

FY 2017
President's Budget Submission

February 9, 2016

Table of Contents

Section 1 – Purpose

1A – Mission Statement
To ensure that national banks and federal savings associations operate in a safe and sound manner, provide fair access to financial services, treat customers fairly, and comply with applicable laws and regulations.

1.1 – Resource Detail Table

Dollars in Thousands

| Office of the Comptroller of the Currency | | FY 2015 | | FY 2016 | | FY 2017 | | FY 2016 to FY 2017 | | | |
Budgetary Resources		Actual		Estimated		Estimated		$ Change		% Change	
	FTE	AMOUNT	FTE	AMOUNT	FTE	AMOUNT	FTE	AMOUNT	FTE	AMOUNT	
Revenue/Offsetting Collections											
Assessments	0	1,110,311	0	1,169,500	0	1,200,900	0	31,400	.00	2.68%	
Interest	0	16,701	0	19,400	0	20,000	0	600	.00	3.09%	
Other Income	0	18,632	0	15,600	0	15,900	0	300	.00	1.92%	
Unobligated Balances from Prior Years	0	1,301,636	0	1,451,369	0	1,522,569	0	71,200	.00	4.91%	
Total Revenue/Offsetting Collections		2,447,280		2,655,869		2,759,369		103,500		3.90%	
Expenses/Obligations											
Supervise	3,337	873,414	3,469	993,905	3,469	1,013,782	0	19,877	0 00%	2.00%	
Regulate	396	103,574	411	117,863	411	120,221	0	2,358	0 00%	2.00%	
Charter	72	18,922	75	21,532	75	21,963	0	431	0 00%	2.00%	
Total Expenses/Obligations	3,805	995,910	3,955	1,133,300	3,955	1,155,966	0	22,666	0 00%	2.00%	
Net Results		1,451,369		1,522,569		1,603,403		80,834		5.31%	

1B – Vision, Priorities, and Context
The Office of the Comptroller of the Currency (OCC) was created by Congress in 1863 to charter national banks; oversee a nationwide system of banking institutions; and ensure national banks are safe and sound, competitive and profitable, and capable of serving in the best possible manner the banking needs of their customers. Effective on July 21, 2011, Title III of the Dodd-Frank Wall Street Reform and Consumer Protection Act (Dodd-Frank Act), transferred to the OCC the responsibility for the supervision of federal savings associations and rulemaking authority for all savings associations.

As of September 30, 2015, the OCC supervised 1,010 national bank charters and 49 federal branches of foreign banks in the United States with total assets of approximately $10.4 trillion, and 416 federal savings associations (which include 165 mutual institutions) with total assets of approximately $688 billion. In total, the OCC supervises approximately $11.1 trillion in financial institution assets.

OCC Vision, Core Values, and Goals

Vision

The OCC is a preeminent prudential bank supervisor that adds value through proactive and risk based supervision; is sought after as a source of knowledge and expertise; and promotes a vibrant and diverse banking system that benefits consumers, communities, businesses, and the U.S. economy.

The OCC culture is agile, accountable, strategy-based, and data-driven. The OCC team of dedicated professionals uses substantive expertise, sound judgment, and comprehensive experience to assess the financial condition, management, and regulatory compliance of national banks and federal savings associations to ensure a vibrant and diverse banking system that benefits all Americans.

Core Values
- **Integrity** – We do the right thing by acting in accordance with law and applicable policies and applying the highest ethical standards.
- **Expertise** – We continuously enhance our skills and experience, act on careful analysis, and apply our knowledge and capabilities to achieve the agency's mission.
- **Collaboration** – We include diverse stakeholders in our decision-making process, seek alternative perspectives, and excel in a team environment.
- **Independence** – We act without undue external influences and exercise our own judgment in a manner consistent with the agency's mission and vision.

Goals

The OCC has established three goals outlined in its strategic plan that help support a strong economy for the American public: 1) A vibrant and diverse system of national banks and federal savings associations that supports a robust U.S. economy; 2) "One OCC" focused on collaboration, innovation, coordination, and process efficiency; 3) The OCC is firmly positioned to continue to operate independently and effectively into the future. To achieve its goals and objectives, the OCC organizes its activities under three programs: 1) Supervise, 2) Regulate, and 3) Charter. Effective supervision and a comprehensive regulatory framework are the key tools that the OCC uses to ensure that national banks and federal savings associations operate in a safe and sound manner and that they provide fair access to financial services and fair treatment of their customers. A robust chartering program allows new entrants into the financial services sector while ensuring that they have the necessary capital, managerial, and risk management processes to conduct activities in a safe and sound manner.

The OCC's priorities focus on strengthening the resiliency of the institutions subject to its jurisdiction through its supervisory and regulatory programs and activities. A stronger and more resilient banking system directly supports three of the Department of the Treasury's (Treasury) FY 2014-2017 strategic goals: Goal 1) Promote domestic economic growth and stability while continuing reforms of the financial system; Goal 4) Safeguard the financial system and use financial measures to counter national security threats; and Goal 5) Create a 21st-century approach to government by improving efficiency, effectiveness, and customer interaction.

The OCC's nationwide staff of bank examiners conducts on-site reviews of banks and provides sustained supervision of these institutions' operations. Examiners analyze asset quality, capital adequacy, earnings, liquidity, and sensitivity to market risk for all banks, and assess compliance with federal consumer protection laws and regulations.[1] Examiners also evaluate management's ability to identify and control risk, and assess banks' performance in meeting the credit needs of the communities in which they operate, pursuant to the Community Reinvestment Act.

In supervising banks, the OCC has the power to:
- Examine banks;
- Approve or deny applications for new charters, branches, capital, or other changes in corporate or banking structure;
- Take supervisory and enforcement actions against banks that do not comply with laws and regulations or that otherwise engage in unsafe or unsound practices;
- Remove and prohibit officers and directors, negotiate agreements—both formal (i.e., public) and informal (i.e., non-public)—to change banking practices, and issue cease-and-desist orders as well as Civil Money Penalties (CMP); and
- Issue rules and regulations, legal interpretations, supervisory guidance, and corporate decisions governing investments, lending, and other practices.

Operations are funded primarily (approximately 97 percent) from semiannual assessments levied on national banks and federal savings associations. Revenue from investments in Treasury securities and other income comprise the remaining three percent of the OCC's funding. The OCC does not receive congressional appropriations to fund any portion of its operations.

Supervisory Activities
The OCC influences the banking system using several means: 1) policy guidance and regulations that set forth standards for sound banking practices; 2) on-site examinations and ongoing off-site monitoring that enable the OCC to assess compliance with those standards and to identify emerging risks or trends; and 3) a variety of supervisory and enforcement tools – ranging from matters requiring the attention of the financial institution's board and management to informal and formal enforcement actions – that are used to obtain corrective action to remedy weaknesses, deficiencies, or violations of law.

The OCC undertook the following initiatives in fiscal year (FY) 2015:
- The OCC published revised procedures providing additional clarity to examiners and bankers about the OCC's policies and procedures for Matters Requiring Attention.
- The OCC and other federal agencies in partnership with the State Liaison Committee of the Federal Financial Institutions Examination Council (FFIEC) issued guidance on private student loans with graduated repayment terms at origination.
- The OCC in conjunction with FFIEC members issued updates to the Bank Secrecy Act/Anti-Money Laundering (BSA/AML) Examination Manual.
- The OCC issued its fall and spring *Semiannual Risk Perspective* reports that discuss

---

[1] The Consumer Financial Protection Bureau assesses compliance with Federal consumer financial laws as defined under Title X of the Dodd Frank Act for banks with assets over $10 billion.

emerging risks facing OCC-supervised banks and identifies supervisory priorities.

- The OCC provided testimony to the Committee on Banking, Housing and Urban Affairs of the United States Senate on cybersecurity and participated in interagency initiatives to improve cybersecurity awareness.
- The OCC and other FFIEC members issued a Cybersecurity Assessment Tool (Assessment) that institutions may use to evaluate their risks and cybersecurity preparedness.
- The OCC reviewed and summarized community and midsize banks' practices for measuring interest rate risk to assist bankers in benchmarking their individual bank's practices.
- The OCC, Federal Deposit Insurance Corporation (FDIC) and Board of Governors of the Federal Reserve System (FRB) issued frequently asked questions (FAQs) on 2013 interagency leveraged lending guidance. The FAQs address questions from the industry relating to the implementation of the guidance.
- The OCC emphasized the changing risk environment for indirect auto lending by OCC-supervised institutions and began taking additional supervisory actions and acquiring additional analytical tools to monitor and assess this risk.
- The OCC monitored the direct and correlated risk to OCC-supervised banks from the rapid decline in crude oil prices.
- The OCC issued its annual *Survey of Credit Underwriting Practices* report, which highlights a continued easing in underwriting standards and an increasing level of policy exceptions.
- The OCC conducted hundreds of outreach meetings with bankers to ensure that the banking industry understands OCC perspectives and expectations.
- The OCC coordinated with the FDIC, FRB, Financial Stability Oversight Council (FSOC), and Basel-related committees on supervisory policies and strategies.
- The OCC continued implementing recommendations from the OCC's international peer review by selecting a Deputy Comptroller for Supervision Risk Management, expanding lead expert groups, and establishing a team to develop an enterprise risk management function for the agency.

In FY 2015, the OCC published on its web site enforcement actions against regulated institutions, including the imposition of CMPs. The OCC continues to be actively involved in the residential foreclosure oversight process to ensure that all foreclosures are handled consistent with regulatory requirements. In addition, over the past year, the OCC took significant enforcement actions to address BSA/AML violations, and unfair, deceptive, or abusive acts or practices.

The OCC's supervisory activities in FY 2015 continued to focus on evaluating and strengthening the quality of banks' risk management to identify, measure, monitor, and control the build-up of risk, both on and off-balance sheet. A primary focus of on-site supervisory activities was the quality of banks' risk management and corporate governance practices. Specific areas of supervisory activities included: 1) evaluating the effectivness of credit risk rating systems, and the adequacy of underwriting standards and allowance for loan and lease reserve methodologies; 2) assessing banks' strategic and business making decision processes to determine that banks comprehensively identify, assess and report all risks arising from cost reduction programs, use of third party vendors, and expansion into new products or services; 3) evaluating banks' interest rate risk exposures and model assumptions; and 4) identifying and controlling cybersecurity threats.

Operational risk management – managing the risk of loss due to (i) failure of people, processes, and systems, and (ii) external events – has become an area of heightened risk and supervisory attention. Strong enterprise risk management processes have been and will continue to be a point of emphasis, particularly at larger institutions. In addition, the OCC continues to assess and address supervisory issues in the areas of fair lending, consumer protection, BSA/AML, and information security.

In addition to its ongoing supervisory activities, the OCC undertook the following initiatives in FY 2015:

- *Final Risk Retention Rule:* The OCC and five federal agencies approved a final rule requiring sponsors of securitization transactions to retain risk in those transactions. The final rule implements the risk retention requirements in the Dodd-Frank Act. The final rule generally requires sponsors of asset-backed securities (ABS) to retain not less than five percent of the credit risk of the assets collateralizing the ABS issuance. As required by the Dodd-Frank Act, the final rule defines a "qualified residential mortgage" (QRM) and exempts securitizations of QRMs from the risk retention requirement. The final rule aligns the QRM definition with that of a qualified mortgage as defined by the Consumer Financial Protection Bureau (CFPB). The final rule also does not require any retention for securitizations of commercial loans, commercial mortgages, or automobile loans if they meet specific standards for high quality underwriting.

- *Large and Midsize Bank Supervision Peer Review:* The OCC continued work on implementing a number of action items as part of its effort to enhance bank and thrift supervision processes and policies. These efforts are the result of an assessment of the OCC's approach to the supervision of large-and mid-sized institutions conducted in 2014 by an international peer review team. Actions completed in FY 2015 included the expansion and realignment of the OCC's lead expert examiners in the agency's Large Bank program; enhancements to the OCC's strategy development process; updates and revisions to the OCC's strategic framework; the establishment of formal Strategic Management and Enterprise Risk Management units; and the enhancements to the analytical functions within the OCC's National Risk Committee structure.

- *Community Bank Regulatory Burden:* The OCC continued its efforts to address concerns regarding regulatory burden on community banks and to foster the ability of small banks to compete in the market place. These efforts included:
  - *The Economic Growth and Regulatory Paperwork Reduction Act Reviews.* The OCC, the FRB, and the FDIC published two notices requesting comment on their regulations and held a series of outreach meetings as part of the agencies' effort to reduce regulatory burden as required by the Economic Growth and Regulatory Paperwork Reduction Act of 1996 (EGRPRA). These notices and outreach meetings provided interested parties an opportunity to comment on regulatory burden reduction directly to the agencies' staff members and senior management.

- *Call Report Simplification.* Through the FFIEC, the OCC, FRB and FDIC commenced a project to consider ways to further tailor reporting requirements for community banks. As part of this effort the agencies plan to undertake a comprehensive review of every line item of every schedule in the Call Report to identify data items that can be deleted and to consider the merits of creating a more streamlined Call Report for certain community banks that would omit schedules and data items not applicable to most of these institutions.
- *Community Bank Collaboration.* The OCC issued a paper entitled "An Opportunity for Community Banks: Working Together Collaboratively," describing how community banks can pool resources to obtain cost efficiencies and leverage specialized expertise. The paper explores the benefits of collaboration, outlines how community banks can structure collaborative arrangements, and emphasizes the need for effective oversight of collaborative arrangements.

- *Independent Foreclosure Review (IFR):* The OCC and the FRB previously amended consent orders against 15 mortgage servicers for deficient practices in mortgage servicing and foreclosure processing. During FY 2015, servicers covered by mortgage servicing and foreclosure related consent orders continued to take action to correct deficiencies in mortgage servicing and foreclosure processes as directed by the OCC and FRB enforcement actions. Servicers reported that much of that work was complete and federal examiners continued the process of verifying and testing that work. In addition, pursuant to the amended consent orders that resolved the IFR, nearly $3.6 billion in payments to eligible borrowers under the settlement funds supervised by the OCC and FRB will have been cashed or deposited through the end of November 2015. In June 2015, the OCC announced that it had terminated the consent orders for three mortgage servicers because it was determined that these institutions complied with the orders issued in April 2011 and amendments issued in February 2013. At the same time, the OCC issued amended orders for six other institutions to restrict certain business activities that they conduct because they have not met all of the requirements of the consent orders. Foreclosure-related consent orders against two other mortgage servicers were terminated previously by operation of law after these institutions ceased to operate as regulated, insured depository institutions. The OCC also announced it will escheat at the end of 2015 any remaining uncashed payments made pursuant to the IFR Payment Agreement so eligible borrowers and their heirs may claim the funds through their states' escheatment processes.

- *Matters Requiring Attention:* The OCC published revised policy and procedures for how it manages Matters Requiring Attention (MRA) resulting from its examination of supervised institutions. MRAs communicate specific supervisory concerns identified during examinations in writing to boards and management teams of regulated institutions. MRAs must receive timely and effective corrective action by bank management and follow-up by OCC examiners. The OCC's updated MRA guidance enhances the agency's ability to ensure a safe and sound federal banking system by emphasizing timely detection and sustainable corrective action of deficient bank practices before they affect the bank's condition. The updated guidance standardizes MRA terminology, format, follow-up, analysis, and reporting across the agency. The guidance addresses recommendations from the international peer review of the OCC's supervision of large and midsize institutions, which was conducted last year.

- *International Swaps and Derivatives Association's (ISDA) Resolution Stay Protocol in Regulatory Capital and Liquidity Coverage Rules:* The OCC, and the FRB issued an interim final rule to ensure that the treatment of over-the-counter (OTC) derivatives, eligible margin loans, and repo-style transactions under the two agencies' regulatory capital and liquidity coverage ratio rules would be unaffected by the implementation of certain foreign special resolution regimes for financial companies or by a banking organization's adherence to the ISDA's Resolution Stay Protocol. In addition, the interim final rule ensures that the lending limits of affected national banks and federal savings association would be unchanged. The regulatory capital and liquidity coverage ratio rules for banking organizations recognize netting or collateral agreements for OTC derivatives and certain securities financing transactions, so long as the banking organization may terminate positions upon an event of default of the counterparty. The rules provide that the transactions may receive this treatment even though certain U.S. laws, including Title II of the Dodd-Frank Act and the Federal Deposit Insurance Act, may temporarily stay the termination rights

- *Guidance on Private Student Loans with Graduated Repayment Terms at Origination:* The OCC and other federal financial regulatory agencies, in partnership with the State Liaison Committee (SLC) of the FFIEC, issued guidance for financial institutions on private student loans with graduated repayment terms at origination.

- *Minimum Requirements for Appraisal Management Companies*: The OCC and five other federal financial regulatory agencies issued a final rule that implements minimum requirements for state registration and supervision of appraisal management companies (AMCs). The final rule implements amendments to Title XI of the Financial Institution Reform, Recovery, and Enforcement Act of 1989 made by the Dodd-Frank Act. Under the rule, states may elect to register and supervise AMCs. The AMC minimum requirements in the final rule apply to states that elect to register and supervise AMCs.

- *Final Flood Insurance Rules:* The OCC, FDIC, FRB, National Credit Union Administration (NCUA), and Farm Credit Administration (FCA) issued a final rule that implements certain provisions of the Biggert-Waters Flood Insurance Reform Act of 2012 and the Homeowner Flood Insurance Affordability Act of 2014, including the mandatory escrow provisions.

- *Bank Secrecy Act/Anti-Money Laundering:* The OCC in conjunction with the other FFIEC member agencies issued updates to the FFIEC's BSA/AML Examination Manual to incorporate regulatory changes and clarify supervisory expectations in a number of areas. The OCC also issued a statement to clarify its expectations with regard to offering banking services to money services businesses.

- *The OCC National Risk Committee's Semiannual Risk Perspective:* The OCC continued to produce this informative semiannual report that highlights the OCC's perspective on key issues and risks that pose threats to the safety and soundness of banks. The report draws upon the findings of the OCC's supervisory activities and analyses of the banking industry.

- *Cybersecurity Risk Management:* During FY 2015, the OCC, under the Comptroller's leadership as the chair of the FFIEC, continued to raise industry awareness of the threats posed to the financial system by cybersecurity risks. In November 2014, the FFIEC issued observations from the cybersecurity assessment pilot that the OCC and other FFIEC agencies conducted during the summer of 2014. The observations provide questions that senior management and boards of directors can use to evaluate their institution's cybersecurity preparedness. The FFIEC also issued a statement encouraging financial institutions to join Financial Services Information Sharing and Analysis Center as part of their actions to identify, respond to and mitigate cyber threats. In March 2015 the FFIEC issued two statements about ways that financial institutions can identify and mitigate cyber-attacks that compromise user credentials or use destructive software, known as malware. Additionally, the OCC's Senior Critical Infrastructure Officer provided testimony to the Committee on Banking, Housing and Urban Affairs of the United States Senate on the cybersecurity initiatives the OCC and the FFIEC have taken, the avenues in place to share cybersecurity information, and recommendations where legislation may be helpful to enhance information sharing among financial institutions. In June 2015, the FFIEC, on behalf of its members, issued a Cybersecurity Assessment Tool (Assessment) that institutions may use to evaluate their risks and cybersecurity preparedness. OCC examiners will incorporate the Assessment into examinations of national banks, federal savings associations, and federal branches and agencies (collectively, banks) of all sizes beginning in late 2015, with completion expected by 2016. Completion for smaller community banks with an 18-month examination cycle is expected by early 2017, or sooner. While all financial institutions may use the Assessment Tool themselves to evaluate their risks and cybersecurity preparedness, OCC examiners will use the Assessment to supplement examination work to gain an understanding of an institution's inherent risk, risk management practices, and controls related to cybersecurity. The Assessment helps banks and examiners determine a bank's inherent risk profile and level of cybersecurity preparedness. The results may be reviewed to determine whether the bank's cybersecurity maturity levels align with the bank's inherent risk profile. In addition to the Assessment, the FFIEC has also made available resources institutions may find useful, including an executive overview, a user's guide, an online presentation explaining the Assessment, and appendixes mapping the Assessment's baseline items to the *FFIEC Information Technology (IT) Examination Handbook* and to the National Institute of Standards and Technology's (NIST) Cybersecurity Framework.

Enforcement Activities
As needed, the OCC uses its enforcement authority to ensure that national banks and federal savings associations operate in a safe and sound manner and in compliance with laws and regulations. This authority comes in the form of formal and informal enforcement actions.

Through September of FY 2015, the OCC published 107 formal enforcement actions against regulated institutions, resulting in the assessment of just over $1 billion in civil money penalties as well as orders for unquantified consumer reimbursement for unfair billing practices and deceptive marketing. The OCC issued 195 enforcement actions against institution-affiliated parties (IAPs), resulting in the assessment of approximately $1 million in civil money penalties.

Significant enforcement activities in FY 2015 included, among others:

- Actions against banks that failed to maintain effective BSA/AML programs and file complete, timely, and accurate Suspicious Activity Reports (SAR).
- Assessment of $950 million in fines against three national banks for unsafe or unsound practices related to the foreign exchange trading business, involving the manipulation of exchange rates and trading actions potentially detrimental to consumers.
- Actions to ensure servicemembers receive credit protections for non-home loans under the Servicemembers Civil Relief Act.
- Assessment of penalties and orders of restitution to bank customers for unfair and deceptive practices in billing for identity theft protection products, marketing practices related to a debt cancellation product, and resolution of deposit amount discrepancies in customer accounts.

The OCC supervision and enforcement staff also work closely with their CFPB counterparts on matters affecting OCC-regulated entities.

Regulatory Activities

The OCC's strategic objectives emphasize regulatory oversight practices that support national banks' and federal savings associations' ability to compete while maintaining safety and soundness. In addition, the OCC will continue its legal work of analysis and interpretation of national bank and federal savings association powers and authorities.

The OCC devoted a significant amount of resources in FY 2015 to regulatory activities relating to the remaining implementation of the Dodd-Frank Act, as well as the finalization and implementation of the Liquidity Coverage Ratio, and participating on the FSOC. Specific actions included:

- The OCC and five federal agencies approved the final Risk Retention Rule under the Dodd-Frank Act.
- The OCC continued efforts to address concerns regarding regulatory burden in community banks. These efforts include:
  - The EGRPRA Reviews
  - Call Report Simplification
  - Community Bank Collaboration
  - Legislative Proposals
- The OCC and the FRB issued an interim final rule to ensure certain treatment under regulatory capital and liquidity coverage ratio rules would be unaffected by adherence to the ISDA's Resolution Stay Protocol.
- The OCC and five other federal agencies issued the final rule on minimum requirements for appraisal management companies.
- The OCC, FRB, FDIC, NCUA, and FCA issued the final flood insurance rules.
- The OCC, FRB, and FDIC finalized revisions to the advanced approaches capital rules adopted in July 2013.

Charter Activities

The OCC processed 2,524 corporate applications and notices in FY 2015, of which 97 percent were completed within required timeframes. In order to address potential safety and soundness problems before they arise, the OCC may impose conditions upon bank transaction approvals covering, for example, capital and liquidity arrangements and deviations from business plans. The OCC continues to receive and process a significant share of applications involving resolution of problem financial institutions.

FY 2016 and 2017 Priorities

A major focus of the OCC's supervisory, regulatory, and administrative programs for FY 2016 will be implementing the remaining applicable provisions of the Dodd-Frank Act and the enhanced capital framework under Basel III. Work will also continue to fully integrate the applicable regulatory, supervisory policy and examination platforms for national banks and federal savings associations and to ensure that these institutions comply with applicable new statutory and regulatory requirements. In addition, the OCC and the other federal banking agencies are conducting a review of the burden imposed on community institutions by existing regulations pursuant to the decennial review required by the EGRPRA.

The OCC is observing signs that credit risk is building, including erosion in the underwriting standards for syndicated leveraged loans and loosening of standards in the indirect auto market. Therefore, the OCC will continue to closely evaluate current underwriting standards by conducting targeted underwriting examinations and completing the annual underwriting survey. The OCC will be working to complete the implementation of recommended actions arising out of the Large and Midsize Supervision Peer Review project and will also continue efforts to implement its strategic initiatives to make the OCC a stronger and more effective organization.

The OCC will conduct examinations based on the risk profile of individual national banks and federal savings associations to ensure they are safe and sound, sufficiently capitalized, and comply with consumer protection laws and regulations. Priorities and activities will include supervisory reviews related to corporate governance and oversight, credit underwriting, compliance, cyber threats, operational risk, BSA/AML, and fair access. Examiners will work to resolve problem national banks and federal savings associations situations effectively by identifying problems at the earliest possible stage, clearly communicating concerns and expectations to bank management through appropriate enforcement actions, and ensuring timely follow-up on needed corrective actions.

Industry Outlook

The environment continues to be challenging for the OCC and the national banking and federal savings association industry ("federal banking system"). The federal banking system faces heightened compliance, operational, reputation, and strategic risks because of significant changes in laws, regulations, and accounting standards. National banks and federal savings associations will need to incorporate these changes into their operations, which is likely to lead to fundamental shifts in many institutions' business models and strategic plans. National banks and federal savings associations also face intense competition and risks from the normalization of interest rates. To address these challenges, the OCC will need to conduct ongoing assessments of emerging risks and the underlying condition of the federal banking system, and to prioritize and allocate resources to the areas and institutions at highest risk.

The federal banking system has weathered a serious disruption to financial markets, a crisis in the mortgage sector, and a slow recovery from a long and deep recession. The long-term trend of consolidation in the federal banking system is likely to continue; the table below shows estimates of the change in number of institutions and share of assets held by banks with over $10 billion in assets, extrapolating from trends experienced between 2004 and 2014. The extrapolations exclude trust companies and foreign branch offices because, compared to national banks and federal savings associations, their growth is less closely linked to underlying domestic economic trends. The asset forecast assumes that system assets continue to grow at the recent average rate of nominal Gross Domestic Product (GDP) over the next five years.

	Number of institutions		Assets	Share of total system assets in institutions with assets >$10 billion	
	OCC banks	OCC thrifts	All OCC-supervised	2014	92.6%
Estimated change 2014 to 2019	-23%	-21%	24%	2019	94.9%

Loan growth has been slower than usual in an economic recovery, in part because the economy as a whole grew more slowly than is usual after a severe recession. The combination of recession and financial crisis caused households to deleverage, reducing loan demand, especially the demand for residential mortgage loans. Tighter underwriting standards have also reduced the supply of credit from pre-recession levels. Commercial lending, however, has been growing, with outstanding commercial and industrial loans now above the pre-recession peak. This has occurred despite firms' large cash reserves, and the ability of medium-size firms to borrow long-term at low rates in bond markets.

Credit loss rates for the system rose sharply for all major loan categories during the financial crisis and recession, but are now back to or below their two-decade averages for all major loan categories. To strengthen their positions in the aftermath of the crisis, many financial institutions have raised additional capital and the largest have built up historically high shares of liquid assets. The result is a stronger federal banking system than existed before the crisis.

Section 2 – Budget Adjustments and Appropriations Language

2.2 – Operating Levels Table

Dollars in Thousands

Office of the Comptroller of the Currency Object Classification	FY 2015 Actual	FY 2016 Estimated	FY 2017 Estimated
11.1 - Full-time permanent	502,530	546,445	557,374
11.3 - Other than full-time permanent	6,672	7,052	7,193
11.5 - Other personnel compensation	3,096	3,255	3,320
11.9 - Personnel Compensation (Total)	**512,298**	**556,752**	**567,887**
12.0 - Personnel benefits	215,491	246,911	251,849
13.0 - Benefits for former personnel	40	149	152
Total Personnel Compensation and Benefits	**$727,829**	**$803,812**	**$819,888**
21.0 - Travel and transportation of persons	55,613	70,695	72,109
22.0 - Transportation of things	2,441	2,271	2,316
23.1 - Rental payments to GSA	56	58	59
23.2 - Rental payments to others	62,848	62,305	63,551
23.3 - Communication, utilities, and misc charges	12,151	16,488	16,818
24.0 - Printing and reproduction	579	718	732
25.1 - Advisory and assistance services	36,307	34,287	34,973
25.2 - Other services	17,991	21,246	21,671
25.3 - Other purchases of goods & serv frm Govt accounts	10,535	12,653	12,906
25.4 - Operation and maintenance of facilities	4,716	4,946	5,045
25.7 - Operation and maintenance of equip	54,249	60,265	61,470
26.0 - Supplies and materials	6,447	7,836	7,993
31.0 - Equipment	20,502	18,675	19,049
32.0 - Land and structures	46	16,750	17,085
42.0 - Insurance claims and indemnities	240	295	301
Total Non-Personnel	**284,721**	**329,488**	**336,078**
Total Budgetary Resources	**$1,012,550**	**$1,133,300**	**$1,155,966**
Budget Activities:			
Supervise	873,414	993,905	1,013,782
Regulate	103,574	117,863	120,221
Charter	18,922	21,532	21,963
Total Budgetary Resources	**$995,910**	**$1,133,300**	**$1,155,966**
FTE	**3,805**	**3,955**	**3,955**

2B – Appropriations Language and Explanation of Changes
The OCC receives no appropriations from Congress.

2C – Legislative Proposals
The OCC has no legislative proposals.

Section 3 – Budget and Performance Plan

3A – Supervise
($993,905,000 from reimbursable resources):
An effective supervision program is the cornerstone of the OCC's activities that support its strategic goals. Specifically, the Supervise Program consists of ongoing supervision and enforcement activities that directly support the OCC's strategic goals to 1) ensure that each national bank and federal savings association is operating in a safe and sound manner and is complying with applicable laws, rules, and regulations relative to the financial institution and the customers and communities it serves, and 2) provide fair access to financial services and fair treatment of customers. Assessing the condition and risk management practices of national banks and federal savings associations, and requiring corrective actions when weaknesses are found, directly supports Treasury's goal of repairing and reforming the financial system.

The OCC's Supervision Program specifically supports the following Treasury Objectives:
1.3: Complete implementation of financial regulatory reform initiatives and continue monitoring the markets for threats to stability;
1.4: Facilitate commerce by providing trusted and secure U.S. currency, products, and services for use by the public;
4.3: Improve the cybersecurity of our Nation's financial sector critical infrastructure; and
4.4: Protect the integrity of the financial system by implementing, promoting, and enforcing anti-money laundering and counterterrorism financing standards.

The primary goal of the OCC's Supervision Program is to ensure that institutions operate in a safe and sound manner and in compliance with laws requiring fair treatment of their customers and fair access to credit and financial products. The OCC's Supervision Program supports the implementation of the financial regulatory reform initiatives including those in the Dodd-Frank Act as well as other regulatory initiatives designed to strengthen the nation's federal banking system. The OCC also monitors risks and threats to the stability of the federal banking system through its regular examinations of the institutions it supervises and other monitoring programs such as its Semi-annual Risk Perspectives Report, participation in the Shared National Credit Program, and its Credit Underwriting Survey.

The OCC's Supervision Program supports facilitating commerce through the goal of ensuring the safety and soundness of the federal banking system. Through its Supervision Program the OCC has taken a number of steps to improve the cybersecurity of the nation's financial sector critical infrastructure including organizing webinars for community bankers. The agency continues to update examiner handbooks, procedures, and training materials to ensure that, as threats evolve, all national banks and federal savings associations can identify cyber risks and strengthen their risk management and control systems. The OCC is an active member of the Financial Services Information Sharing and Analysis Center, which provides greater real-time insight into a broad range of potential threats to the industry and the ability to assist, when appropriate, in a coordinated response with other government agencies. Finally, the OCC supports protecting the integrity of the financial system through its examinations of compliance with BSA/AML and through the initiation of enforcement actions for non-compliance with BSA/AML laws and regulations.

Description of Performance:
Percentage of National Banks and Federal Savings Associations with Composite CAMELS Rating of 1 or 2:
The composite Capital Adequacy, Asset Quality, Management, Earnings, Liquidity, and Sensitivity (CAMELS) rating reflects the overall condition of a national bank or federal savings association. Bank regulatory agencies use the Uniform Financial Institutions Rating System, CAMELS, to provide a general framework for evaluating all significant financial, operational, and compliance factors inherent in a national bank or federal savings association. The rating scale is 1 through 5 of which 1 is the highest rating granted. These CAMELS ratings are assigned at the completion of every supervisory cycle or when there is a significant event leading to a change in CAMELS.

The OCC has established a target outcome measure that 90 percent of the institutions under its supervision have a composite CAMELS rating of 1 or 2. Such a rating is consistent with the strategic goal of a safe and sound banking system, that banks maintain adequate capital and liquidity and have strong risk management practices. As of September 30, 2015, 91 percent of national banks and federal savings associations earned composite CAMELS ratings of either 1 or 2. Degradation in CAMELS can reflect weaknesses in risk management systems that need corrective action. The OCC, consistent with Treasury's goal of repairing and reforming the financial system and supporting the recovery of the housing market, has instructed bank examiners to identify and seek corrective action at an earlier stage to address potential problems or weaknesses. The OCC's primary focus is to ensure that CAMELS ratings are an accurate reflection of each institution's current financial position, and thus the OCC would not take action to prematurely restore a favorable CAMELS rating. As national bank or federal savings association performance and asset quality improves and directed corrective actions are implemented, the OCC expects CAMELS ratings to continue to improve.

Percentage of National Banks and Federal Savings Associations that are Considered Well-Capitalized:
The Federal Deposit Insurance Act established a system that classifies insured depository institutions into five categories (well capitalized, adequately capitalized, undercapitalized, significantly undercapitalized, and critically undercapitalized) based on their capital levels relative to their risks. The OCC has established a target outcome measure that 95 percent of national banks and federal savings associations will meet or exceed the well-capitalized threshold.

The economic environment and resulting increase in problem assets placed a strain on some banks' capital buffers that has resulted in levels below the OCC's target performance measure. The OCC works closely with problem national banks and federal savings associations to develop rehabilitation plans. Such plans typically include directives to improve or restore capital levels. These efforts, combined with a more stable operating environment, have resulted in improvement in this performance goal since FY 2009. As of September 30, 2015, 95 percent of national banks and federal savings associations were classified as well capitalized.

Percentage of National Banks and Federal Savings Associations with Consumer Compliance Rating of 1 or 2:

To ensure fair access to financial services and fair treatment of national bank and federal savings association customers, the OCC evaluates an institution's compliance with consumer laws and regulations. Bank regulatory agencies use the Uniform Financial Institutions Rating System, Interagency Consumer Compliance Rating, to provide a general framework for evaluating significant consumer compliance factors inherent in an institution. Each institution is assigned a consumer compliance rating based on an evaluation of its present compliance with consumer protection and civil rights statutes and regulations, and the adequacy of its operating systems designed to ensure continuing compliance. Ratings are on a scale of 1 through 5 of which 1 is the highest rating granted. The target for FY 2015 and FY 2016 will currently remain unchanged at 94 percent. As of September 30, 2015, national banks and federal savings associations continue to show strong compliance with consumer protection regulations with 96 percent earning a consumer compliance rating of either 1 or 2. Under the Dodd-Frank Act, the OCC has enforcement and supervisory authority for those institutions with total assets of no more than $10 billion.

Rehabilitated National Banks and Federal Savings Associations as a Percentage of Problem National Banks and Federal Savings Associations One Year Ago:

The OCC's primary goal for problem national banks and federal savings associations can reach a point at which rehabilitation is no longer feasible. The OCC's early identification and intervention with problem financial institutions can lead to a successful rehabilitation. As of September 30, 2015, 39 percent of national banks and federal savings associations with composite CAMELS ratings of 3, 4, or 5 one year ago have improved their ratings to either 1 or 2 this year. This is aligns with the target of 40 percent for FY 2015. The OCC continues to focus on the early identification and rehabilitation of problem institutions.

As previously noted, the OCC is taking a number of steps through its Supervise and Regulate programs to make national banks and federal savings associations more resilient to financial stresses and to identify and obtain corrective action at an earlier stage, when problems can be addressed most successfully. These efforts include heightened capital and liquidity standards and increased emphasis on the need for stress testing, designed to provide financial institutions with stronger capital buffers to withstand unforeseen events. These are multi-year efforts that will continue in FY 2015 and beyond.

Total OCC Costs Relative to Every $100,000 in National Bank and Federal Savings Association Assets Regulated:

Beginning in FY 2006, the OCC implemented a performance measure that reflects the efficiency of its operations while meeting the increasing supervisory demands of a growing and more complex federal banking system.

The OCC costs are those reported as total program costs on the annual audited Statement of Net Cost. National bank and federal savings association assets are those reported quarterly by national banks and federal savings associations on the Reports of Condition and Income. Total national bank and federal savings association assets represent the growth and complexity of the financial institutions under the jurisdiction of the OCC. This measure supports the OCC's strategic goal of efficient use of agency resources. The OCC's ability to control its costs while ensuring the safety and soundness of national banks and federal savings associations benefits all national bank and federal savings association customers. As of September 30, 2015, total OCC cost relative to every $100,000 in assets regulated was $9.37 compared to the FY 2015 target of $10.20. The OCC will continue its efforts to ensure that resources are used prudently and that programs are carried out in a cost effective manner.

3.1.1 – Supervise Budget and Performance Plan

Dollars in Thousands

Supervise Budget Activity

Resource Level	FY 2010 Actual	FY 2011 Actual	FY 2012 Actual	FY 2013 Actual	FY 2014 Actual	FY 2015 Actual	FY 2016 Estimated	FY 2017 Estimated
Expenses/Obligations	$618,254	$684,273	$924,417	$873,942	$889,111	$873,414	$993,905	$1,013,782
Budget Activity Total	**$618,254**	**$684,273**	**$924,417**	**$873,942**	**$889,111**	**$873,414**	**$993,905**	**$1,013,782**

Measure	FY 2010 Actual	FY 2011 Actual	FY 2012 Actual	FY 2013 Actual	FY 2014 Actual	FY 2015 Actual	FY 2016 Target	FY 2017 Target
Percent of National Banks and Federal Savings Associations with Composite CAMELS Rating 1 or 2	N/A	N/A	76.0	80.0	87.0	91.0	90.0	90.0
Percentage of National Banks and Federal Savings Associations That Are Categorized As Well Capitalized	N/A	N/A	92.0	94.0	93.0	95.0	95.0	95.0
Percentage of National Banks and Federal Savings Associations With Consumer Compliance Rating of 1 or 2	N/A	N/A	93.0	94.0	95.0	96.0	94.0	94.0
Rehabilitated National Banks And Federal Savings Associations As A Percentage Of Problem National Banks One Year Ago (CAMEL 3,4, or 5)	N/A	N/A	27.0	34.0	39.0	39.0	40.0	40.0
Total OCC Costs Relative To Every $100,000 in Bank And Federal Savings Associations Assets Regulated ($)	N/A	N/A	10.51	9.99	9.75	9.37	10.20	10.20

Key: DISC - Discontinued

3B – Regulate

($117,863,000 from reimbursable resources):
The OCC's Regulate Program specifically supports the following Treasury Objectives:
1.3: Complete implementation of financial regulatory reform initiatives and continue monitoring the markets for threats to stability;
1.4: Facilitate commerce by providing trusted and secure U.S. currency, products, and services for use by the public; and
4.4: Protect the integrity of the financial system by implementing, promoting, and enforcing anti-money laundering and counterterrorism financing standards.

The Regulate Program supports the OCC's strategic goal of a vibrant and diverse system of national banks and federal savings associations that supports a robust U.S. economy. Specifically, the Regulate Program consists of ongoing activities that result in the establishment of regulations, policies, operating guidance, and interpretations of general applicability to national banks and federal savings associations. These regulations, policies, and interpretations may establish system-wide standards, define acceptable national banking and federal savings association practices, provide guidance on risks and responsibilities facing national banks and federal savings associations, or prohibit (or restrict) national banking or federal savings association practices deemed to be imprudent or unsafe. They also establish standards for ensuring fair access to financial services and fair treatment of national bank and federal savings association customers. This program includes establishing examination policies and handbooks; interpreting administrative, judicial, and congressional proceedings; and establishing the applicable legal and supervisory framework for new financial services and products.

Description of Performance:
Specific activities undertaken in FY 2015 as part of this program were described earlier and included the issuance of various supervisory guidance on the Volcker rule, heightened enterprise risk management expectations, and third party relationship management. Significant resources also were spent on various Dodd-Frank rulemakings, including those pursuant to section 171(b) regarding minimum risk-based capital requirements; section 941 pertaining to risk retention requirements and associated minimum underwriting standards for asset securitizations; and sections 731 and 764 related to capital requirements and margin requirements on certain swap transactions. In FY 2015, the OCC continued to support operations of the FSOC and issue Dodd-Frank rulemakings.

3.1.2 – Regulate Budget and Performance Plan

Dollars in Thousands

Regulate Budget Activity

Resource Level	FY 2010 Actual	FY 2011 Actual	FY 2012 Actual	FY 2013 Actual	FY 2014 Actual	FY 2015 Actual	FY 2016 Estimated	FY 2017 Estimated
Expenses/Obligations	$97,735	$108,171	$125,416	$111,783	$105,436	$103,574	$117,863	$120,221
Budget Activity Total	**$97,735**	**$108,171**	**$115,416**	**$111,783**	**$105,436**	**$103,574**	**$117,863**	**$120,221**

3C – Charter
($21,532,000 from reimbursable resources):
The OCC's Charter Program specifically supports the following Treasury Objectives:
1.4: Facilitate commerce by providing trusted U.S. currency, products, and services for use by the public;
4.4: Protect the integrity of the financial system by implementing, promoting, and enforcing anti-money laundering and counterterrorism financing standards.

The Charter Program consists of ongoing activities that result in the chartering of national banks and federal savings associations and the evaluation of the permissibility of structures and activities of national banks and federal savings associations and their subsidiaries. This includes the review and approval of new national bank and federal savings association charters, federal branches and agencies, mergers, acquisitions, conversions, business combinations, corporate reorganizations, changes in control, operating subsidiaries, branches, relocations, and subordinated debt issuances. By supporting the entry of new products and institutions into the financial system in a manner consistent with safety and soundness, the Charter Program supports the OCC's strategic goals of assuring safety and soundness while allowing national banks and federal savings associations to offer a full competitive array of financial services.

Description of Performance:

Percentage of Licensing Applications and Notices Completed within Established Time Frames: The OCC's timely and effective approval of corporate applications contributes to the nation's economy by enabling national banks and federal savings associations to complete various corporate transactions and introduce new financial products and services. Delays in providing prompt decisions on applications and notices can deprive a national bank or federal savings association of a competitive or business opportunity, create business uncertainties, or diminish financial results. Time frames have been established for completing each type of application and notice. As of September 30, 2015, the OCC completed 97 percent of national bank and federal savings association applications and notices within the required time frame, above the target of 95 percent. The OCC will continue to meet its Charter Program goals by providing staff training, coordination between charter and supervisory staff on safety and soundness and compliance matters, issuance of updated procedures, and maintaining an emphasis on accessibility and early consultation with national bank and federal savings association organizers and others proposing national bank and federal savings association structure changes.

3.1.3 – Charter Budget and Performance Plan

Dollars in Thousands

Charter Budget Activity								
Resource Level	FY 2010 Actual	FY 2011 Actual	FY 2012 Actual	FY 2013 Actual	FY 2014 Actual	FY 2015 Actual	FY 2016 Estimated	FY 2017 Estimated
Expenses/Obligations	$24,434	$27,043	$27,338	$30,486	$19,262	$18,922	$21,532	$21,963
Budget Activity Total	**$24,434**	**$27,043**	**$27,338**	**$30,486**	**$19,262**	**$18,922**	**$21,532**	**$21,963**

Measure	FY 2010 Actual	FY 2011 Actual	FY 2012 Actual	FY 2013 Actual	FY 2014 Actual	FY 2015 Actual	FY 2015 Target	FY 2016 Target	FY 2017 Target
Percentage of Licensing Applications and Notices Completed within Established Timeframes	N/A	N/A	98.0	97.0	98.0	97.0	95.0	95.0	95.0

Key: DISC - Discontinued

Section 4 – Supplemental Information

4A – Summary of Capital Investments

The OCC's IT strategic plan aligns information technology initiatives and investments to the OCC's core mission, including the development of new or enhanced applications and services and the disposition of redundant or "end-of-lifecycle" applications, capabilities, and services.

The IT strategic plan is implemented through the budget formulation and the Capital Planning and Investment Control processes. These processes ensure that all IT investments are aligned with the OCC's mission, goals, objectives, and target enterprise architecture before a project is funded. The capital planning process reviews and prioritizes detailed business cases to promote technology reuse, to capitalize on enterprise opportunities, and to reduce redundant and obsolete capabilities and services. Invest, evaluate, and control ensures that the OCC IT strategy has adequate funding and staff resources to address IT investment priorities, and considers risk mitigation strategies for IT investments that are not meeting stated cost, time, and performance goals. Performance metrics are linked to the delivery, alignment, and achievement of the OCC's strategic program objectives. Cost effectiveness for each investment is evaluated through regular benchmarking studies, featuring peer group organizations. Key metrics used to evaluate infrastructure include availability, reliability, utilization, defects, and customer satisfaction.

FY 2016 and 2017 Plans

The OCC has 3 major IT initiatives in FY 2016 and 2017:

Servers Support Services (SSS) - The SSS supports the OCC's server Operations and Maintenance. The infrastructure staff continues to build out additional capacity at the co-location facility to support the server technology refresh, business resiliency, and increases in enterprise storage capacity. In addition, a managed disaster recovery services contract will be initiated to implement a proven, highly reliable, secure, expandable, and cost-effective disaster recovery solution for OCC's critical business systems.

Telecommunications Services and Support (TSS) - TSS includes telecommunications wide area network and local area network infrastructure. Remote access to the OCC systems is facilitated via a virtual private network, dial-in, and cellular wireless access using two-factor authentication. This also includes messaging services supporting highly mobile bank examiners and the OCC staff. In FY 2016, the OCC will continue an on-going effort to upgrade the headquarters and field office phone systems and telecom infrastructure including Local Area Network/Wide Area Network hardware, Video Tele-Conferencing and Voice Over Internet Protocol.

End User Services and Support (EUSS) - The EUSS includes help desk/customer service support, personal computer hardware and software operations and maintenance, asset management, and desktop engineering and image management. New computers and peripherals will be deployed to a portion of the workforce in FY 2016. In FY 2016, the OCC will also refresh hand-held devices.

A summary of capital investment resources, including major information technology and non-technology investments, can be viewed and downloaded at: http://www.treasury.gov/about/budget-performance/Pages/summary-of-capital-investments.aspx. This website also contains a digital copy of this document.

www.ingramcontent.com/pod-product-compliance
Lightning Source LLC
Chambersburg PA
CBHW080534190526
45169CB00008B/3168